THE BATTLE OF
SHILOH

Surprise Attack!

By **Larry Hama** Illustrated by **Scott Moore**

New York

Published in 2007 by The Rosen Publishing Group, Inc.
29 East 21st Street, New York, NY 10010

First edition, 2007

Photo Credits: p. 4 National Archives and Records Administration; p. 5 (top) Courtesy of the Library of Congress, p. 5 (bottom) National Archives and Records Administration; p. 7 (top) Courtesy of the Library of Congress, (bottom) National Archives and Records Administration; p. 44 Courtesy of the Library of Congress, p. 45 (top) Courtesy of the Tennessee State Library and Archives, (bottom) National Archives and Records Administration

Simone Drinkwater, Series Editor/Osprey Publishing
Nel Yomtov, Series Editor/Rosen Book Works
Karl Bollers, Editor/Rosen Book Works

Library of Congress Cataloging-in-Publication Data

Hama, Larry.
    The Battle of Shiloh: surprise attack! / by Larry Hama.— 1st ed.
    p. cm. — (Graphic battles of the Civil War)
    Includes bibliographical references and index.
    ISBN-13   978-1-4042-0779-0 (lib.)   978-1-4042-6478-6 (pbk.)
    ISBN-10   1-4042-0779-1 (lib.)   1-4042-6478-7 (pbk.)
    6-pack ISBN-13   978-1-4042-6274-4   6-pack ISBN-10 1-4042-6274-1
    1. Shiloh, Battle of, Tenn., 1862—Juvenile literature. I. Title. II. Series.

E473.54.H36 2007
973.7'31—dc22

                                                                2006007309

CONTENTS

THE AMERICAN CIVIL WAR, 1861 – 1865

By the middle of the nineteenth century, there were important economic and political differences between the Northern and Southern states in America. None was more important than the issue of slavery. The South depended upon slave labor to work its plantations. Slavery was illegal in the North.

These differences led to anger between the North and South. In 1860, Abraham Lincoln, an antislavery candidate, won the presidential election. The South believed that their way of life would be destroyed. Shortly after the election, South Carolina seceded, or left, the Union. More Southern states seceded. They formed the Confederate States of America, a separate government.

Tensions grew. Finally, on April 12, 1861, Southern forces bombed Fort Sumter, in South Carolina. About one year later, an important battle was fought near Shiloh, Tennessee. The winner of that battle gained much-needed dominance in a key region of the war.

KEY COMMANDERS

ULYSSES S. GRANT
Commander of the Union Army of the Tennessee. By 1864, he commanded all Union armies. Grant was President Lincoln's favorite general. He later became president.

ALBERT S. JOHNSTON
Commander of the Confederate Army of the Mississippi at Shiloh. In 1861, he refused Lincoln's offer to command the Union army and joined the South instead.

WILLIAM T. SHERMAN
Commmanded a division of Grant's Union army at Shiloh, and then later commanded all Union forces in the West.

PIERRE G. T. BEAUREGARD
Johnston's second-in-command at Shiloh. He took command when Johnston was killed. Later, he commanded forces in the West.

3

By the start of the American Civil War, the United States was divided into three parts. They were the eleven states of the Confederate States of America, or Confederacy, the nineteen states of the Union, and the four states that had declared themselves neutral. These

★ **General Ulysses S. Grant**

★ *Union general Ulysses S. Grant was the most experienced general at the battle of Shiloh. He became one of the greatest generals in history.*

four states were Delaware, Kentucky, Maryland, and Missouri.

Missouri and Kentucky were particularly important. They controlled the northern part of the Mississippi River, which could give the Union access to the heart of the Confederacy. If these

states joined the South, Confederate armies would be within striking distance of the Midwest. Both sides began recruiting militias in the two states.

Fighting began first in Missouri in May 1861. Union troops drove the Confederates out of the state by August. In September, Confederate general Leonidas Polk decided, against his government's wishes, to occupy southwestern Kentucky. The state legislature then declared Kentucky pro-Union and appealed for Union-supporting troops. Polk's superior, General Albert Sidney Johnston, had no choice but to support Polk with the rest of his forces.

Johnston had a problem. He didn't have enough troops to seize or hold Kentucky. He concentrated on keeping Union armies from three main waterways. A fort at Columbus, Kentucky, blocked the Mississippi, and Forts Henry and Donelson covered the Cumberland and Tennessee rivers. The rest of Johnston's command occupied the railroad junction of Bowling Green, Kentucky.

Johnston's opponent was Union general Henry Halleck. Halleck's larger force was in Missouri. General Don Carlos Buell led a smaller force at Louisville, Kentucky. Neither army had much training. Weapons were in short supply. One of Halleck's generals, Ulysses S. Grant, proposed an immediate attack on Forts Henry and Donelson. Halleck reluctantly agreed.

★ *Union soldiers were happily enjoying their Sunday breakfast when attacking Confederate forces caught them by surprise.*

★ *General Albert Sidney Johnston was considered by Confederate president Jefferson Davis the nation's most able officer.*

Grant, supported by a small fleet of river gunboats, first captured Fort Henry on February 6, 1862. Alarmed, Johnston left Bowling Green and sent half his troops to Fort Donelson. However, Grant successfully laid siege to that fort on February 12. The Confederates surrendered. Grant became a national hero for his part in the first major Union victory of the war.

Johnston then moved his troops at Columbus down the Mississippi to the newly constructed fortress of Island No. 10.

Halleck now divided his command. General John Pope was to attack down the Mississippi and capture the fortress of Island No. 10. Meanwhile, Grant's Army of the Tennessee would pursue Johnston down the Tennessee to his base at Corinth, Mississippi. Buell's Army of the Ohio would join him to take it. Buell decided to first occupy Nashville. Then, when ready, he would join up with Grant.

Grant advanced on Corinth in March 1862. He camped near Pittsburg Landing, on the west bank of the Tennessee River. Grant's main concern was to train his troops and link up with Buell.

Five of Grant's six divisions camped together. However, no one scouted the area, sent out patrols, or dug defensive trenches. Johnston saw his chance. Assembling five different forces at Corinth, he planned to destroy Grant before Buell could join him. Johnston left the details to his second-in-

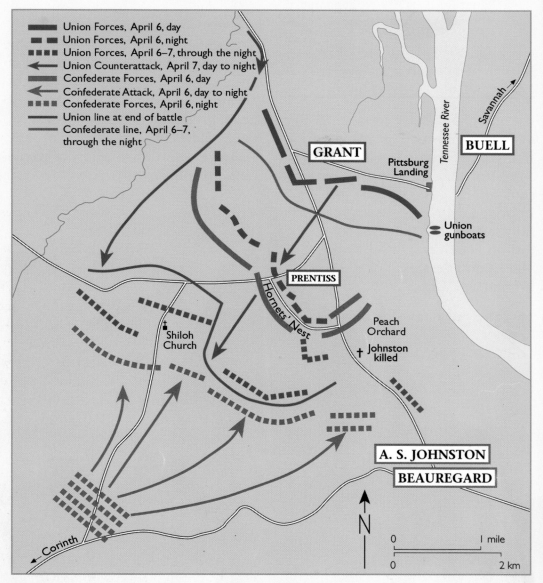

Union Forces, April 6, day
Union Forces, April 6, night
Union Forces, April 6–7, through the night
Union Counterattack, April 7, day to night
Confederate Forces, April 6, day
Confederate Attack, April 6, day to night
Confederate Forces, April 6, night
Union line at end of battle
Confederate line, April 6–7, through the night

GRANT

BUELL

Pittsburg Landing

Tennessee River

Savannah →

Union gunboats

PRENTISS

Hornets' Nest

Peach Orchard

Shiloh Church

Johnston killed

A. S. JOHNSTON

BEAUREGARD

Corinth

N

0   1 mile
0   2 km

★ *Confederate generals Johnston and Beauregard planned a sneak attack on Grant's troops that were camped at Pittsburg Landing. Grant wanted to attack the Confederates at their base in Corinth. Both plans were ruined when soldiers from both sides met by accident, halfway between the two camps at the Hornets' Nest on July 6. Once the battle began, Union and Confederate troops rushed to join the fight.*

★ **General Benjamin Prentiss**

★ *Confederate Brigadier General Benjamin Prentiss was a strong, spirited leader. However, he had to surrender his men at Shiloh.*

command, General P. T. Beauregard.

The 23-mile approach march took three days. Orders were confused and units got mixed up. Rains turned the roads to mud. Beauregard told Johnston to forget the attack completely. Johnston ordered it anyway. He would attack at dawn, April 6, 1862.

Beauregard need not have worried. Unaware of the surprise to come, Union soldiers prepared breakfast in their camps. Only Colonel Everett Peabody was alarmed at reports of Confederate troops nearby. He ordered a search party. They found more Confederates than they could have imagined. The fight was on.

The Army of the Mississippi attacked in three waves. They first hit General Benjamin Prentiss's camp, overrunning it. William Tecumseh Sherman's division fought briefly, but was also driven back.

★ *Union troops fled the Shiloh battlefield on steamboats that were docked on the Tennessee River.*

Union battle lines quickly formed as more troops came up. The untrained units were horribly unprepared. Many Union soldiers fled. Union general Stephen Hurlbut's division came up. They took cover in a sunken road, which they held. Union generals Prentiss and W. H. L. Wallace and the remains of their divisions joined them. They, too, held the Confederate advance. Sherman also held.

Beauregard's attack plan had resulted in total confusion. Commanders had lost control of their forces. Johnston went forward to press the attack toward the river. Beauregard, left in charge, sent the last reserves into the general confusion. While leading an attack on the Peach Orchard, Johnston was killed.

Confederate general Dan Ruggles brought up artillery guns and opened fire directly into the sunken road. Prentiss, the senior surviving Union commander, surrendered two hours later. The Confederates pushed on, but the final Union line held. The last of Grant's divisions finally reached the battlefield. Troops from Buell's Union Army of the Ohio were also arriving from across the river. This battle would prove to be deadly for both sides.

THE BATTLE OF SHILOH: SURPRISE ATTACK!

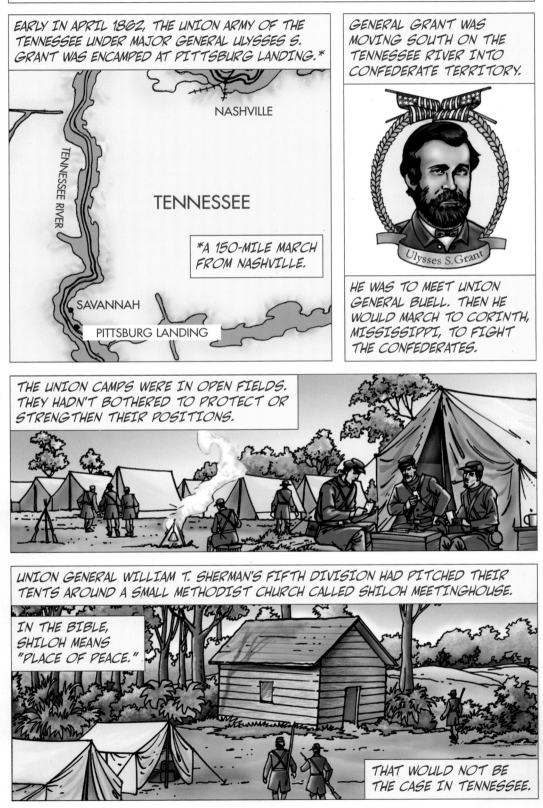

EARLY IN APRIL 1862, THE UNION ARMY OF THE TENNESSEE UNDER MAJOR GENERAL ULYSSES S. GRANT WAS ENCAMPED AT PITTSBURG LANDING.*

NASHVILLE

TENNESSEE RIVER

TENNESSEE

*A 150-MILE MARCH FROM NASHVILLE.

SAVANNAH

PITTSBURG LANDING

GENERAL GRANT WAS MOVING SOUTH ON THE TENNESSEE RIVER INTO CONFEDERATE TERRITORY.

Ulysses S. Grant

HE WAS TO MEET UNION GENERAL BUELL. THEN HE WOULD MARCH TO CORINTH, MISSISSIPPI, TO FIGHT THE CONFEDERATES.

THE UNION CAMPS WERE IN OPEN FIELDS. THEY HADN'T BOTHERED TO PROTECT OR STRENGTHEN THEIR POSITIONS.

UNION GENERAL WILLIAM T. SHERMAN'S FIFTH DIVISION HAD PITCHED THEIR TENTS AROUND A SMALL METHODIST CHURCH CALLED SHILOH MEETINGHOUSE.

IN THE BIBLE, SHILOH MEANS "PLACE OF PEACE."

THAT WOULD NOT BE THE CASE IN TENNESSEE.

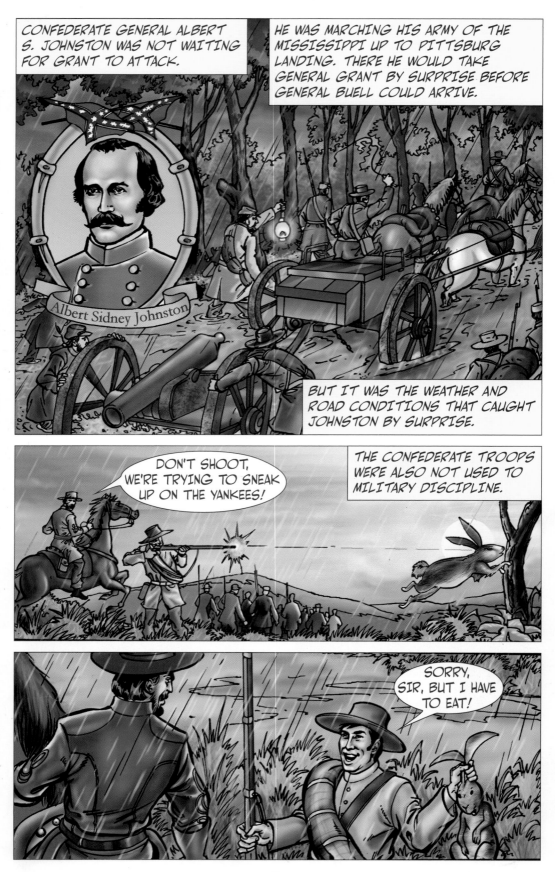

MANY OF THE UNION TROOPS WERE NEW AND UNTRAINED.

... THIS IS THE END YOU PUT THE BULLET IN.

SOME HAD BEEN GIVEN THEIR RIFLES ONLY TEN DAYS BEFORE.

MANY MEN IN THE VOLUNTEER REGIMENTS BELIEVED THAT THE WAR WAS GOING TO BE A GRAND ADVENTURE.

SOME SOLDIERS BROUGHT THEIR DOGS WITH THEM FROM HOME.

GOOD BOY, REX!

GRANT WAS A NATIONAL HERO AFTER HIS VICTORY AT FORT DONELSON. HE WAS FEELING SURE OF HIMSELF.

THERE WILL BE NO FIGHTING AT PITTSBURG LANDING. WE WILL HAVE TO GO TO CORINTH.

HIS HORSE HAD FALLEN ON HIS LEG EARLIER IN THE WEEK.

ONE OF GRANT'S BRIGADE COMMANDERS, COLONEL PEABODY, WAS NOT AS CONFIDENT. HE SENT OUT A SCOUTING MISSION.

AT 3:00 A.M. ON APRIL 6, UNION MAJOR JAMES POWELL LED THREE COMPANIES OF THE 25TH MISSOURI SOUTH TO "TAKE A LOOK-SEE."

JUST BEFORE SUNRISE, CONFEDERATE GENERAL BEAUREGARD, JOHNSTON'S SECOND-IN-COMMAND, WAS CONCERNED AS WELL.

SIR, WE HAVE LOST ALL CHANCE OF SURPRISING THE ENEMY! WE HAVE HEARD THEIR BANDS PLAYING AND THEIR CHEERS ...

... I FEAR THAT BUELL HAS REINFORCED GRANT AND WE ARE WALKING INTO A TRAP!

WHAT'S THAT SHOOTING?

SHORTLY AFTER 5:00 A.M., THEY WERE INTERRUPTED BY THE SOUND OF MUSKET FIRE FROM THE NORTH.

THE BATTLE HAS BEGUN, GENTLEMEN ...

... TONIGHT WE WATER OUR HORSES IN THE TENNESSEE RIVER!

THE MUSKET FIRE HEARD BY GENERAL JOHNSTON WAS COMING FROM FRALEY'S FIELD, WHERE POWELL'S MISSOURI SCOUTS WERE SHOOTING IT OUT WITH THE 3RD MISSISSIPPI.

TELL GENERAL PRENTISS AT DIVISION HEADQUARTERS THAT THE ENEMY IS HERE IN FORCE!

IMMEDIATELY, WORD WAS SENT TO GRANT AND ALL THE DIVISIONAL COMMANDERS.

PRENTISS WAS ENRAGED AT PEABODY FOR ORDERING THE MISSION. "I WILL HOLD YOU PERSONALLY RESPONSIBLE FOR THIS ENGAGEMENT!" HE SHOUTED.

GENERAL SHERMAN WAS NOT TOO ALARMED ...

SIR, THE REBS ARE OUT THERE THICKER THAN FLEAS ON A DOG!

YOU MUST BE BADLY SCARED OVER THERE.

THE OHIO BOYS HELD OUT FOR TWO ASSAULTS BY THE 6TH MISSISSIPPI. THEY INFLICTED TERRIBLE CASUALTIES ...

... BUT ON THE THIRD ASSAULT, FEELING OUTNUMBERED, APPLER FELT IT WOULD BE WISE TO BE CAUTIOUS.

RETREAT, AND SAVE YOURSELVES!

THE BATTLEFIELD, 9:00 A.M., APRIL 6.

GENERAL JOHNSTON WAS DRIVING THE UNION FORCES INTO A DEAD END FORMED BY OWL CREEK, SNAKE CREEK, AND THE TENNESSEE RIVER.

SNAKE CREEK

TENNESSEE RIVER

OWL CREEK

HURLBUT

SHERMAN

JOHNSTON

PRENTISS

PITTSBURG LANDING

JOHNSTON

MOST OF PRENTISS'S DIVISION WAS IN RETREAT. MAJOR POWELL AND COLONEL PEABODY WERE BOTH DEAD.

GRANT RUSHED DOWN FROM HIS HEADQUARTERS. IT WAS A NINE-MILE TRIP BY STEAMBOAT.

HE HAD ALREADY ALERTED BUELL TO SPEED UP HIS ARMY OF THE OHIO'S MARCH TO PITTSBURG LANDING.

THREE MILES UPRIVER, GRANT PASSED UNION GENERAL LEW WALLACE AT CRUMP'S LANDING.

GENERAL WALLACE! GET YOUR TROOPS UNDER ARMS AND READY TO MOVE!

THEY ALREADY ARE, SIR!

MOST OF SHERMAN'S DIVISION HAD ABANDONED THEIR ENCAMPMENT AT SHILOH MEETINGHOUSE AND WERE FORMING UP A SECOND LINE OF DEFENSE.

NEVER GOT TO FINISH BREAKFAST!

SOME REBEL IS FINISHING IT FOR YOU!

A HEADQUARTERS AIDE ASKED SHERMAN FOR A REPORT.

TELL GRANT IF HE HAS ANY MEN TO SPARE, I CAN USE THEM. IF NOT, I WILL DO THE BEST I CAN.

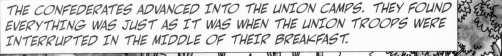

THE CONFEDERATES ADVANCED INTO THE UNION CAMPS. THEY FOUND EVERYTHING WAS JUST AS IT WAS WHEN THE UNION TROOPS WERE INTERRUPTED IN THE MIDDLE OF THEIR BREAKFAST.

THE CONFEDERATES HAD STARTED THEIR MARCH WITH THREE DAYS' RATIONS. THEY ATE IT ALL ON THE FIRST DAY.

THIS MORNING FOUND THEM VERY HUNGRY, INDEED.

STOMACHS FULL, THE CURIOUS CONFEDERATES STARTED LOOKING THROUGH THEIR ENEMY'S THINGS.

MY! THIS FELLOW'S GOT **TWO** SWEETHEARTS!

ONE OF 'EM'S HIS **MAMA**, YOU FOOL!

THE ASSAULT DWINDLED TO A STOP.

DON'T STOP NOW! WE MUST CONTINUE THE ATTACK!

GRANT RODE OFF FROM PITTSBURG LANDING WITH HIS CRUTCH STRAPPED TO HIS SADDLE.

UNION GENERALS W. H. L. WALLACE* AND HURLBUT REPORTED THEIR ACTIONS TO GRANT.

SIR, WE HAVE RE-FORMED RANKS AND ARE SENDING REINFORCEMENTS TO OUR FAR LEFT.

DON'T LET THE CONFEDERACY OUTFLANK US, GENERAL WALLACE!

*NOT TO BE CONFUSED WITH GENERAL LEW WALLACE.

SHERMAN'S DIVISION HAD RE-FORMED AT ITS SECOND POSITION.

MY BIGGEST WORRY IS RUNNING OUT OF AMMUNITION, SIR!

MORE IS ON THE WAY!

UNION GENERAL JOHN MCCLERNAND'S DIVISION WAS HOLDING THE LINE NORTH OF SHILOH MEETINGHOUSE ...

... AND GRANT SEEMED TO BE EVERYWHERE AT ONCE!

GRANT REDIRECTED ARTILLERY, ORGANIZED SCATTERED POCKETS OF HIS INFANTRY, GOT ONE HORSE SHOT OUT FROM UNDER HIM, FOUND A REPLACEMENT, AND KEPT RIDING.

A CONFEDERATE BULLET TORE HIS HAT FROM HIS HEAD. HE CONTINUED WITHOUT A HAT.

ANOTHER BULLET BLEW THE INSIGNIA OFF HIS SHOULDER.

ANOTHER SPENT BULLET LODGED IN HIS COAT POCKET.

HE THREW IT AWAY CASUALLY, AND HIS TROOPS CHEERED.

AT THE FAR LEFT OF THE UNION LINE, GRANT FOUND THE 6TH DIVISION HARD-PRESSED BUT HOLDING FIRM.

COMMANDING THE 6TH WAS BRIGADIER GENERAL BENJAMIN PRENTISS ...

Benjamin Prentiss

THEY WERE MAKING A STAND IN A TRENCH FORMED BY A SUNKEN FARM LANE THAT RAN ALONG THE EDGE OF SOME HEAVY WOODS.

... WHO NO LONGER HAD PEABODY AND POWELL TO BLAME FOR HIS PROBLEMS.

YOU ARE HOLDING OUR LEFT FLANK, SIR. YOU WILL MAINTAIN THIS POSITION AT ALL HAZARDS!

I WILL TRY, SIR!

THEY'RE COMING BACK FOR MORE, BOYS! LET'S GIVE IT TO THEM!

BEHIND THE CONFEDERATE LINES, GENERAL JOHNSTON CAME ACROSS ONE OF HIS LIEUTENANTS LOOTING.

NONE OF THAT, SIR. WE ARE NOT HERE FOR PLUNDER.

JOHNSTON THEN REALIZED THAT HE HAD MADE THE SOLDIER FEEL BAD AFTER THE MAN HAD RISKED HIS LIFE ON HIS ORDERS.

LET THIS BE MY SHARE OF THE SPOILS TODAY!

IT WAS A SIMPLE TIN CUP. FROM THAT MOMENT ON, HE USED IT INSTEAD OF HIS SWORD TO DIRECT THE BATTLE.

LATER, WHEN ASSAULT AFTER ASSAULT ON THE UNION LEFT HAD FAILED, JOHNSTON USED THE CUP AGAIN.

MEN, THEY ARE STUBBORN ...

... WE MUST USE THE BAYONET.

THE TROOPS COULD DO NO LESS THAN FOLLOW HIM INTO THE DEADLY FIRE OF THE PEACH ORCHARD.

I WILL LEAD YOU!

BUT HURLBUT'S MEN HAD REACHED THEIR LIMIT AND WITHDREW. THIS LEFT THE ORCHARD TO THE CONFEDERATES.

GENERAL, ARE YOU HURT?

YES, AND I FEAR SERIOUSLY.

A BULLET HAD ENTERED JOHNSTON'S LEG, CUTTING A MAJOR ARTERY ...

... AND HE BLED TO DEATH FROM A WOUND THAT COULD HAVE BEEN EASILY TREATED ...

... HAD HE NOT ALREADY ORDERED HIS STAFF PHYSICIAN TO ATTEND TO THE UNION WOUNDED.

21

He had told the doctor, "These men were our enemies a moment ago. They are our prisoners now. Take care of them."

Command of the Army of the Mississippi fell to General G. T. Beauregard.

He had been in the rear during all the fighting and had no clear picture of what was going on.

Beauregard made the mistake of sending his chief of staff, Colonel Thomas Jordan, up to the front.

Jordan considered himself a keen tactical thinker. He had no doubts about putting theory into practice.

MARCH TOWARD THE SOUND OF THE HEAVIEST FIRING!

The men who obeyed Jordan's orders walked into the very areas where the most Union guns were aimed. The Confederates were mowed down instantly.

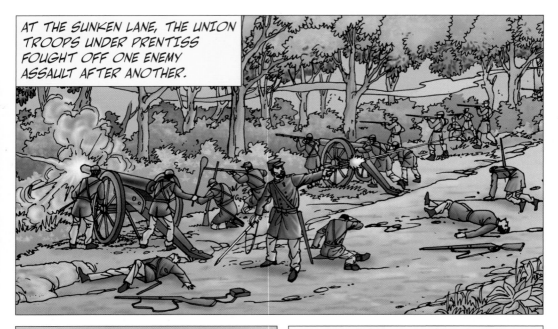

AT THE SUNKEN LANE, THE UNION TROOPS UNDER PRENTISS FOUGHT OFF ONE ENEMY ASSAULT AFTER ANOTHER.

SIR, IF WE FALL BACK NOW, WE CAN SAVE WHAT'S LEFT OF OUR DIVISION!

I WAS ORDERED TO MAINTAIN THIS POSITION AT ALL HAZARDS, AND I INTEND TO DO SO.

SAMUEL CARRICO OF THE 61ST ILLINOIS WAS SO INEXPERIENCED THAT HE THOUGHT THAT THE CONSTANT BUZZING AND "ZIPS" OF BULLETS WERE BEES.

CONFEDERATE TROOPS CONTINUED TO CHARGE THE SUNKEN LANE DESPITE MASSIVE LOSSES.

ONE OF THE CONFEDERATE COLONELS LEADING THE ATTACK SAID, "IT WAS A PERFECT RAIN OF BULLETS, SHOT, AND SHELL."

A CONFEDERATE PRIVATE REPORTED THAT "...THE DEFENDERS MOWED US DOWN WITH EVERY VOLLEY."

IT'S LIKE A HORNETS' NEST IN THERE!

THE NAME STUCK. THE SUNKEN LANE AT SHILOH HAS BEEN KNOWN EVER SINCE AS "THE HORNETS' NEST."

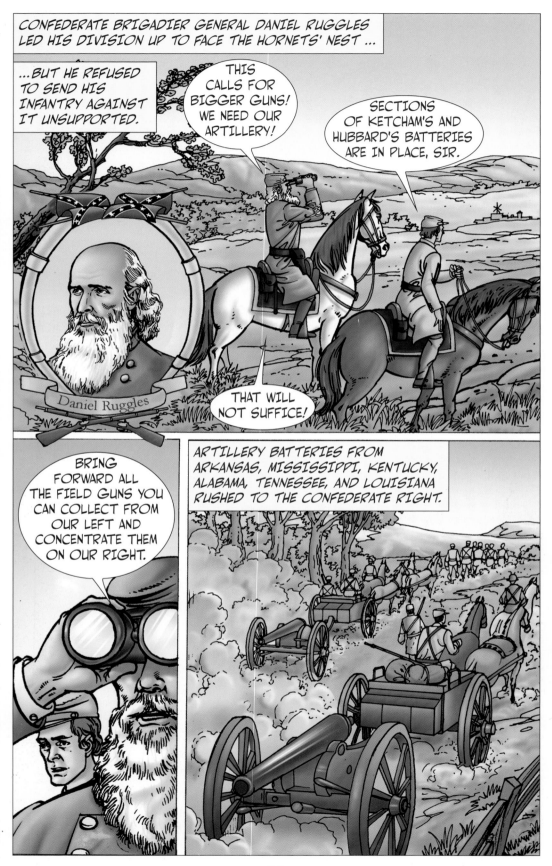

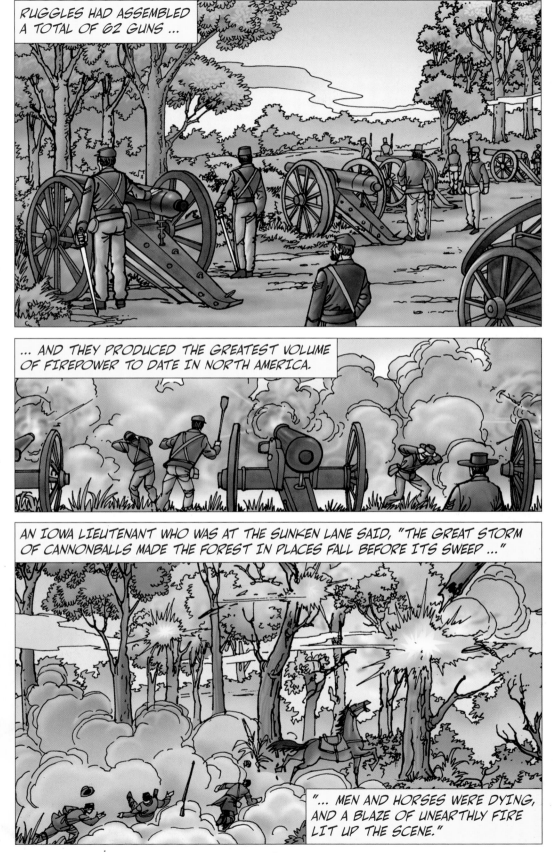

RUGGLES HAD ASSEMBLED A TOTAL OF 62 GUNS ...

... AND THEY PRODUCED THE GREATEST VOLUME OF FIREPOWER TO DATE IN NORTH AMERICA.

AN IOWA LIEUTENANT WHO WAS AT THE SUNKEN LANE SAID, "THE GREAT STORM OF CANNONBALLS MADE THE FOREST IN PLACES FALL BEFORE ITS SWEEP ..."

"... MEN AND HORSES WERE DYING, AND A BLAZE OF UNEARTHLY FIRE LIT UP THE SCENE."

ANN WALLACE, THE WIFE OF GENERAL W. H. L. WALLACE, ARRIVED AT PITTSBURG LANDING FOR A SURPRISE VISIT AND FOUND A BATTLE IN PROGRESS.

SHE WAS TOLD THAT THE GENERAL HAD BEEN SEVERELY WOUNDED AND LEFT FOR DEAD ON THE BATTLEFIELD.

I'M DREADFULLY SORRY, MA'AM.

ANN WALLACE SPENT THE REST OF THE DAY NURSING THE WOUNDED. SHE WAITED IN VAIN FOR WORD OF HER HUSBAND.

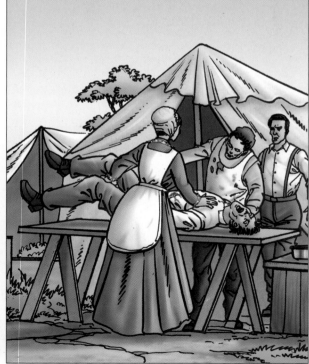

AT THE HORNETS' NEST, UNION TROOPS WERE COMPLETELY PINNED DOWN BY THE FEROCITY OF RUGGLES' ARTILLERY BOMBARDMENT.

WILKINS! I THOUGHT I SENT YOU TO THE REAR WITH THE OTHER WOUNDED.

THERE ISN'T A REAR, CAPTAIN! SOMEBODY GIVE ME A GUN!

THE PRIVATE WAS RIGHT. CONFEDERATE TROOPS WERE MOVING IN ON BOTH SIDES OF PRENTISS'S POSITIONS AND TO HIS REAR.

PRENTISS HAD NOT BUDGED, BUT THE UNITS ON BOTH SIDES OF HIM HAD FLED TO THE RIVER.

THE SITUATION WAS BECOMING CLEAR TO THE DEFENDERS AT THE HORNETS' NEST.

GENERAL PRENTISS, I BELIEVE WE ARE FLANKED AND TRAPPED.

AT 5:16 P.M., PRENTISS SURRENDERED HIS REMAINING 2,200 MEN.

CONFEDERATE COLONEL NATHAN BEDFORD FORREST ACCEPTED PRENTISS'S SURRENDER.

HE HAD STARTED THE DAY WITH 6,000 MEN.

THE CONFEDERATE ATTACK STALLED AS HUNDREDS OF SOLDIERS STAYED BEHIND TO GUARD AND GAPE AT THE CAPTURED UNION SOLDIERS.

THE UNION TROOPS HAD LEFT ALL THEIR POSSESSIONS BEHIND IN THEIR ABANDONED CAMPS.

IT WAS HARD TO RESIST TEMPTATION.

IT SEEMED THAT HALF THE CONFEDERATE ARMY WAS STRUGGLING BACK TO CORINTH LOADED DOWN WITH LOOT.

IN SURRENDERING, PRENTISS MAY JUST HAVE SAVED GRANT AND THE REST OF THE UNION ARMY.

A HALF HOUR BEFORE PRENTISS SURRENDERED, GENERAL "BULL" NELSON'S DIVISION OF BUELL'S ARMY ARRIVED OPPOSITE PITTSBURG LANDING.

Lew Wallace

TWO HOURS LATER, LEW WALLACE TURNED UP, FIVE HOURS LATE FOR THE FIGHT. HE HAD MADE A WRONG TURN.

HE WAS DEEPLY SHAMED BY HIS FAILURE.

BEN HUR

BEN HUR

BY GENRAL LEW WALLAGE

WALLACE WOULD BECOME THE FAMOUS AUTHOR OF *BEN HUR*, BUT HE NEVER WROTE A SINGLE WORD ABOUT WHAT HAPPENED AT SHILOH.

NIGHT FELL. BEAUREGARD STOPPED THE ATTACK. HE HAD HIS EXHAUSTED TROOPS WITHDRAW TO THE FORMER UNION CAMPS.

THAT NIGHT, CROSSING THE MISSISSIPPI RIVER TO PITTSBURG LANDING WITH UNION GENERAL NELSON'S DIVISION WAS SERGEANT AMBROSE BIERCE OF THE 9TH INDIANA. HE LATER WROTE ...

"... ALONG THE SHELTERED STRIP OF BEACH BETWEEN THE RIVER-BANK AND THE WATER WAS A CONFUSED MASS OF HUMANITY, SEVERAL THOUSANDS OF MEN."

"A MORE DEMENTED CREW NEVER DRIFTED TO THE REAR OF BROKEN BATTALIONS."

"THIS ABOMINABLE MOB HAD TO BE KEPT OFF WITH BAYONETS."

NELSON REACTED WITH ANGER RATHER THAN DISGUST.

THEY WERE INSENSIBLE TO SHAME AND SARCASM ...

... I ASKED PERMISSION TO FIRE ON THE KNAVES.

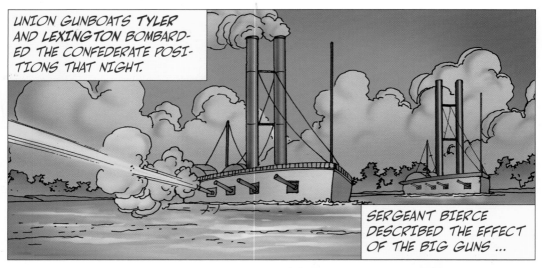

UNION GUNBOATS *TYLER* AND *LEXINGTON* BOMBARDED THE CONFEDERATE POSITIONS THAT NIGHT.

SERGEANT BIERCE DESCRIBED THE EFFECT OF THE BIG GUNS ...

"OBJECTS A MILE AWAY SPRANG TOWARD OUR EYES AS A SNAKE STRIKES AT THE FACE OF A VICTIM ... THE REPORT STUNG US TO THE BRAIN ..."

"... THEN, A SURPRISINGLY LONG TIME AFTERWARD, A DULL DISTANT EXPLOSION, AND A SUDDEN SILENCE OF SMALL-ARMS TOLD THEIR OWN TALE."

FOR THE MOST PART, THE BOMBARDMENT WAS NOT EFFECTIVE, BUT THERE WERE CERTAINLY CASUALTIES ...

THE NEXT MORNING, A GROUP OF CONFEDERATES WERE FOUND DEAD IN A CAPTURED TENT – THEIR PLAYING CARDS STILL GRIPPED IN THEIR HANDS.

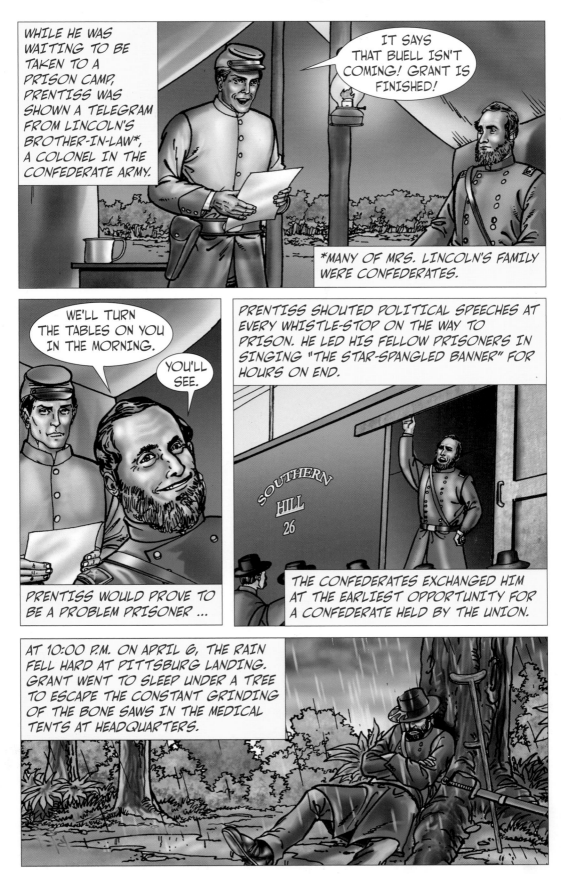

WHILE HE WAS WAITING TO BE TAKEN TO A PRISON CAMP, PRENTISS WAS SHOWN A TELEGRAM FROM LINCOLN'S BROTHER-IN-LAW*, A COLONEL IN THE CONFEDERATE ARMY.

IT SAYS THAT BUELL ISN'T COMING! GRANT IS FINISHED!

*MANY OF MRS. LINCOLN'S FAMILY WERE CONFEDERATES.

WE'LL TURN THE TABLES ON YOU IN THE MORNING.

YOU'LL SEE.

SOUTHERN HILL 26

PRENTISS WOULD PROVE TO BE A PROBLEM PRISONER ...

PRENTISS SHOUTED POLITICAL SPEECHES AT EVERY WHISTLE-STOP ON THE WAY TO PRISON. HE LED HIS FELLOW PRISONERS IN SINGING "THE STAR-SPANGLED BANNER" FOR HOURS ON END.

THE CONFEDERATES EXCHANGED HIM AT THE EARLIEST OPPORTUNITY FOR A CONFEDERATE HELD BY THE UNION.

AT 10:00 P.M. ON APRIL 6, THE RAIN FELL HARD AT PITTSBURG LANDING. GRANT WENT TO SLEEP UNDER A TREE TO ESCAPE THE CONSTANT GRINDING OF THE BONE SAWS IN THE MEDICAL TENTS AT HEADQUARTERS.

BY DAWN ON APRIL 7, ALL THE UNION REINFORCEMENTS WERE IN PLACE. LEW WALLACE, MCCLERNAND, HURLBUT, CRITTENDEN,* AND NELSON FORMED A SOLID LINE WEST-TO-EAST FROM SNAKE CREEK TO THE TENNESSEE.

*PART OF BUELL'S FORCE, HE ARRIVED DURING THE NIGHT.

SHERMAN PUT IT INTO WORDS FOR ALL OF THEM ...

GIVE THEM HELL!

THE CONFEDERATES PUT UP A GOOD FIGHT, BUT BY 1:00 P.M. THE OUTCOME WAS OBVIOUS.

GENERAL BEAUREGARD, WE SHOULD GET AWAY WITH WHAT WE HAVE.

I INTEND TO WITHDRAW IN A FEW MOMENTS.

AT 2:00 P.M., THE ORDER WENT OUT TO THE CONFEDERATE TROOPS. THE RETREAT WAS OFFICIAL. THEY WOULD RETURN TO CORINTH.

THAT NIGHT, A DRENCHING RAIN FELL, THEN FROZEN SLEET, AND THEN HAILSTONES THE SIZE OF PARTRIDGE EGGS.

BEAUREGARD RODE UP AND DOWN THE COLUMN, GIVING COMFORT AND ENCOURAGEMENT TO THE WOUNDED.

THE NEXT MORNING, THE UNION BURIAL PARTIES BEGAN THEIR GRIM TASK. STRETCHER BEARERS BROUGHT WOUNDED FROM BOTH SIDES TO THE SURGEONS' TABLES.

SHERMAN SET OUT WITH A SINGLE BRIGADE* TO PURSUE AND HARASS THE RETREATING CONFEDERATES.

*AT FULL STRENGTH, A BRIGADE IS OVER 4,000 MEN, BUT CASUALTIES HAD REDUCED THEIR SIZE BY AT LEAST HALF.

COLONEL NATHAN BEDFORD FORREST WAS ASSIGNED TO LEAD THE CONFEDERATE REAR GUARD.

Nathan Forrest

HE HAD FEWER THAN FOUR TROOPS OF CAVALRY: 350 HORSEMEN FROM TEXAS, KENTUCKY, TENNESSEE, AND MISSISSIPPI.

AT FALLEN TIMBERS, FORREST DID THE UNEXPECTED WHEN CONFRONTED BY SHERMAN'S BRIGADE, WHICH OUTNUMBERED HIM FIVE TO ONE.

CHARGE!

THE LEADING REGIMENT OF UNION SKIRMISHERS BROKE AND RAN.

CHARGE!

PAST THE SKIRMISHERS, FORREST RAN INTO THE MAIN BODY OF SHERMAN'S BRIGADE ...

CHARGE!

BUT THE OTHERS HAD NOT FOLLOWED HIM. HE WAS ALONE IN THE MIDDLE OF A HOSTILE ARMY.

KILL HIM!

A UNION BULLET TORE INTO FORREST'S SIDE. IT ALMOST UNSEATED HIM FROM HIS SADDLE.

CUTTING A PATH BEFORE HIM WITH HIS SABER, HE HAULED A UNION SOLDIER ONTO THE BACK OF HIS HORSE AND USED HIM AS A SHIELD.

DON'T SHOOT! THAT'S ONE OF OUR BOYS HE'S GOT!

NATHAN BEDFORD FORREST WAS THE LAST MAN WOUNDED AT SHILOH.

HE WOULD BE PROMOTED TO GENERAL AND SURVIVE THE WAR.

ADVANCING UNION TROOPS DISCOVERED GENERAL W. H. L. WALLACE STILL ALIVE. HE WAS TERRIBLY WOUNDED, LYING AMONG THE DEAD AND DYING.

A KIND-HEARTED CONFEDERATE HAD WRAPPED HIM IN A BLANKET.

WALLACE WAS ABLE TO RECOGNIZE HIS WIFE WHEN HE WAS BROUGHT BACK TO THE MEDICAL TENTS ...

ANN...

... BUT HIS HEAD WOUND BECAME INFECTED. HE DIED SHORTLY AFTER.

MRS. WALLACE ARRANGED A DISPLAY OF HIS PORTRAIT, HORSE, AND MILITARY SADDLE OUTSIDE THEIR HOME IN OTTAWA, ILLINOIS.

A TALE IS TOLD OF ANOTHER ILLINOIS WIDOW WHO CAME TO THE BATTLEFIELD IN SEARCH OF HER HUSBAND'S BODY.

I SURE AM SORRY, MA'AM, BUT THE GRAVES ARE MOSTLY UNMARKED.

IT WAS ALL WE COULD DO JUST TO GET THEM ALL UNDERGROUND ...

... NOW, AIN'T THAT THE DARNDEST THING? THAT DOG JUST WON'T LEAVE THAT ONE GRAVE. WE SHOO HIM OFF, BUT HE KEEPS COMING BACK.

WOOF! WOOF!

THE WIDOW RECOGNIZED HER HUSBAND'S DOG IMMEDIATELY ...

... AND THE GRAVE THE FAITHFUL PET STOOD WATCH OVER WAS INDEED HER HUSBAND'S.

AT DAY'S END, THE CASUALTY COUNT AT SHILOH CAME TO OVER 10,000 PER SIDE.

THE UNION LOSSES WERE 1,754 KILLED, 8,408 WOUNDED, AND 2,885 TAKEN PRISONER. THE SOUTH SUFFERED 1,723 DEAD, 8,012 WOUNDED, AND 959 MISSING.

THE COMBINED CASUALTIES OF TWO DAYS' FIGHTING AT SHILOH WERE HIGHER THAN ALL THE CASUALTIES OF ALL PREVIOUS AMERICAN WARS PUT TOGETHER.*

*THE REVOLUTIONARY WAR, THE WAR OF 1812, AND THE MEXICAN WAR.

STILL, GRANT HAD WON A GREAT VICTORY. BUT HIS SUPERIOR, MAJOR GENERAL HENRY HALLECK, WAS NOT PLEASED.

GRANT HAD ALLOWED HIMSELF TO BE SURPRISED, HE HAD NOT BEEN PREPARED, HE HAD NOT FOLLOWED THE RULES, AND HE HAD BEEN LAX IN FILLING OUT HIS PAPERWORK.

HALLECK STORMED DOWN TO PITTSBURG LANDING TO TAKE COMMAND PERSONALLY. HE ALSO SENT A NOTE TO WASHINGTON DEMANDING GRANT'S REMOVAL.

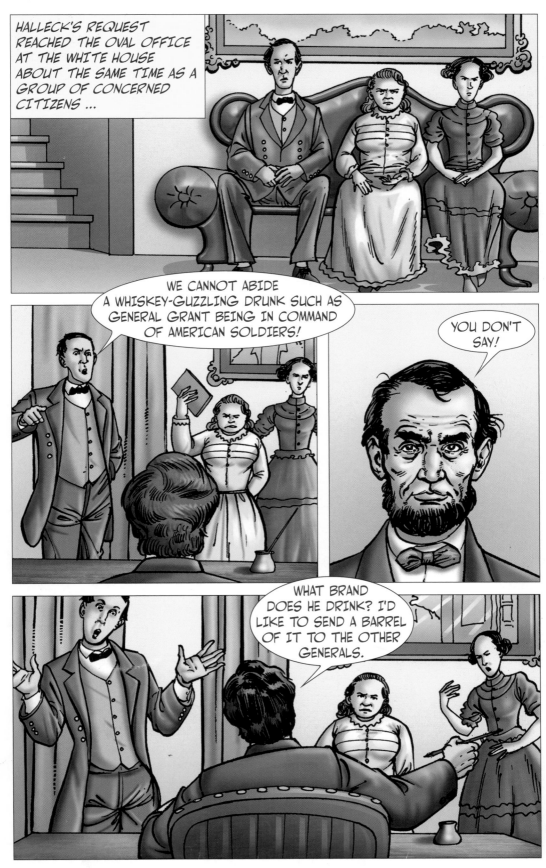

AFTER THE WAR, GENERAL GRANT BECAME THE HERO OF THE NATION. HE EASILY WON THE PRESIDENCY IN 1867.

HE IS BURIED IN A BEAUTIFUL TOMB IN NEW YORK CITY.

GENERAL BEAUREGARD'S REPUTATION AFTER THE WAR WAS RUINED BY HIS ASSOCIATION WITH A LOTTERY SCANDAL IN LOUISIANA.

GENERAL PRENTISS BECAME A LEADER OF THE REPUBLICAN PARTY IN MISSOURI.

PRESIDENT BUCHANAN APPOINTED HIM POSTMASTER.

SERGEANT AMBROSE BIERCE BECAME A FAMOUS WRITER.

AT THE AGE OF 71, HE DISAPPEARED IN MEXICO.

GENERAL SHERMAN IS STILL THE BEST-KNOWN UNION COMMANDER AFTER GRANT. HIS MOST FAMOUS QUOTE IS ...

"... WAR IS HELL."

THE END

43

The Confederates spent a restless night in the captured camps, occasionally bombarded by Union gunboats and artillery. The dead and wounded of both sides lay everywhere around them in the rain. Many soldiers tried to help, but some looted.

Beauregard, reassured that Buell was nowhere nearby, expected to resume the attack in the morning. Instead, a reinforced Grant attacked him.

The Confederates fought back bravely, but it was hopeless. "Our troops are very much in the condition of a lump of sugar, thoroughly soaked with water, preserving its original shape, though ready to dissolve,"

remarked Beauregard's chief of staff. Beauregard, now aware Buell had arrived, ordered a withdrawal to Corinth. The Union army was left with the battlefield, the wounded, and the dead. It was a hot day. The vultures were already at work.

The exhausted Confederates retreated in a seven-mile column. Wagons loaded with wounded made their escape over several hot days and rainy nights. Loot, even cannon, was abandoned. A half-hearted pursuit was repulsed.

Total casualties at Shiloh were 23,741 on both sides. This was more than in all previous wars in North

★ *Confederate soldiers, shown here dressed in many different uniforms, burned their supplies before leaving their camp at Corinth.*

★ *Nathan Bedford Forrest refused to surrender his men at Shiloh and escaped. He became one of the most feared Confederate soldiers.*

New Orleans fell to the Union navy on April 24, opening up the lower Mississippi. Beauregard and his men abandoned Corinth on April 30. Memphis fell to the Union army in June. Now only Vicksburg, Mississippi, held the two halves of the Confederacy together.

However, the South was far from finished, even in the West. Within six months, offensives were launched to regain Corinth and even invade Kentucky. It would take sixteen months to capture Vicksburg. But, after Shiloh, "the Confederacy never smiled again."

America put together. It was also over five times that of First Bull Run, which had shocked the nation a year before.

Nothing had been gained for either side. But the defeat was far worse for the South, with its smaller population. On April 16, the Confederate congress passed a National Conscription Law, for men between 18 and 35.

Meanwhile, the war went on.

On April 4, the night rain falling on Johnston's approach march shielded the Union gunboat *Carondelet* as it ran by the guns of the fortress at Island No. 10. Below the fortress, she joined General John Pope's troops on the Missouri side. Supported by its guns, they crossed the Mississippi River and the fort was cut off. Its men surrendered the day Beauregard retreated from Shiloh. The upper Mississippi was in Union hands.

★ *In order to withdraw quickly from Corinth, Beauregard and his men not only had to burn, but also to abandon valuable supplies.*

★Glossary★

abominable Thoroughly unpleasant or disagreeable.

artery Any of a system of blood vessels that carry blood away from the heart.

artillery Large, heavy guns that are mounted on wheels or tracks.

brigade A large army unit.

company A group of soldiers led by a captain.

conscription Forced enrollment of people for military service.

dwindle To become gradually less until little is left.

engagement A military encounter; a battle.

ferocity The state or quality of being fierce.

harass To carry out repeated attacks and raids against.

infantry The branch of an army trained to fight on foot.

inflict To cause pain or suffering.

knave A dishonest crafty man.

lax Not careful or strict; negligent.

lottery A contest in which tickets are sold, the winning ticket or tickets being determined in a random drawing.

musket A gun with a long barrel used before the invention of rifles.

outflank To maneuver around and behind the flank of an opposing force.

rations Food issued or available to members of a group.

rear guard A military detachment detailed to bring up and protect the rear of a main body or force.

sarcasm A sharply mocking, often ironic remark intended to wound.

scandal Something that offends the morality of the social community.

secede To formally withdraw from a group or organization, often to form another organization.

skirmisher A soldier who engages in a minor fight with a small force of enemy soldiers.

spoils Goods or property seized or robbed, especially after a military victory.

volley A discharge of bullets from a gun.

★ For More Information ★

ORGANIZATION

National Civil War Museum
P.O. Box 1861
Harrisburg, PA 17105-1861
(717) 260-1861

National Park Service
Shiloh National Military Park
1055 Pittsburg Landing Road
Shiloh, TN 38376
(731) 689-5696
Web site: http://www.nps.gov/shil/

FOR FURTHER READING

Arnold, James R. *Shiloh 1862: The Death of Innocence.* Oxford, England: Osprey Publishing, 1998.

Foote, Shelby. *Shiloh.* New York: Vintage Books, 1991.

Grimsley, Mark. *Shiloh: A Battlefield Guide.* Lincoln, NE: Bison Books, 2006.

Time-Life Books, ed. *Shiloh (Voices of the Civil War).* New York: Time-Life Books, 1996.

★Index★

A
abominable, 32
artery, 21
artillery, 7, 18, 25, 28, 44

B
battlefield, 7, 14, 27, 40, 44
Beauregard, P. T., 3, 6–7, 11,
    22, 31, 35–36, 43–45
Bierce, Sergeant Ambrose,
    32–33, 43
brigade, 11, 36–37
Buell, General Don Carlos,
    4–9, 11, 15, 31, 34–35, 44

C
company, 11
conscription, 45
Corinth, 5–8, 10, 30, 36,
    44–45

D
division, 3, 6–8, 12, 14–15,
    17, 19, 23, 25, 31–32
dwindle, 16

E
engagement, 12

F
ferocity, 28
Forrest, Colonel Nathan
    Bedford, 29, 37–38
Fort Donelson, 4–5, 10
Fort Henry, 4–5

G
Grant, Ulysses S., 3–12, 15,
    17–19, 30, 34, 41–44

H
Halleck, General Henry, 4–5,
    41–42
harass, 36
headquarters, 12, 15, 34
Hornets' Nest, 7, 24–25, 28–29

I
infantry, 18, 25
inflict, 14

J
Johnston, Albert Sidney, 3–7,
    9, 11–12, 14, 20, 45

K
knave, 32

L
lax, 41
Lincoln, Abraham, 3, 34
looting, 20, 30, 44
lottery, 43

M
march, 6, 15, 45
Mississippi River, 4–5, 32, 45
Mississippi, Army of the, 3, 7,
    9, 22
musket, 11–12

O
Ohio, Army of the, 5, 7, 15
outflank, 17

P
Peabody, Colonel Everett, 6,
    11–12, 14, 19
Peach Orchard, 7, 21

Pittsburg Landing, 6–10,
    14–15, 17, 27, 31–32, 34,
    41
Polk, General Leonidas, 4
Pope, General John, 5, 45
Prentiss, Brigadier General
    Benjamin, 7, 12, 14, 19,
    23, 28–31, 34, 43

R
rations, 16
rear guard, 37
regiment, 10, 37
reinforcements, 13, 17, 35, 44
retreat, 14, 36, 44–45
Ruggles, General Dan, 7,
    25–26, 28

S
sarcasm, 32
scandal, 43
scout, 6, 11–12
Sherman, William Tecumseh,
    3, 7–8, 12–15, 17, 35–37,
    43
Shiloh Meetinghouse, 8, 15, 17
skirmisher, 13, 37
spoils, 20
sunken road, 7, 19, 23–24, 26

T
Tennessee, 3, 8, 25, 37
Tennessee, Army of the, 3, 5, 8

V
volley, 24

W
Wallace, Major General Lewis,
    31, 35

WEB SITES

Due to the changing nature of Internet links, the Rosen Publishing Group, Inc., has developed an online list of Web sites related to the subject of this book. This site is updated regularly. Please use this link to access the list:

http://www.rosenlinks.com/gbcw/shiloh